OUTSIDE OF HERE.
OUTSIDER HEAR!

By the same author:

Nicked Names (2022)
Japanabandon (2023)
Manifest.oh! (2023)
Diaspora³ (2023)
Objections, Scars & Artefacts (2023)

OUTSIDE OF HERE.
OUTSIDER HEAR!

ANDREW GEOFFREY KWABENA MOSS

RECENT
WORK
PRESS

Outside of here. Outsider hear!
Recent Work Press
Canberra, Australia

ISBN: 9781763670112 (paperback)

A catalogue record for this
book is available from the
National Library of Australia

Cover image: features the Akan Drum held by the British Museum
Cover design: Recent Work Press
Set by Recent Work Press

recentworkpress.com

EF

Mum, Dad & brother Mike

Contents

RHYTHM

Akan Drum Talking

A burst of sudden tempo evokes tremors
Reverberating beyond the walls of the British
Museum, beyond the glass coffin in Room 26

Originally, I came from baphia and cordia africana—the finest grains of hardwood
Carved musically with elegant painful resonances
Treated at first respectfully, housed royally, in a sacred dwelling
Symbolically potent, I accompanied births, deaths and marriages
Played by a griot in the Chief's orchestra until I was traded in

Deer hide skin stretching across a harrowing Middle Passage
Bound for Virginia on a slave ship, six months I travelled, exercising captives:
'dancing the slaves' to my shame I was beat … by slave traders
Bodies shackled together underdeck, packed dense as sardines in cans
Commodities occasionally let up to breathe
Merchandise, like horses and fine cars, kept moving
to fight depression and disease, to keep 'healthy'
Preserved for a life of slave labour, best before their sell-by date

Ushered into a holding pen then on plinth to be sold
On the plantation I was used for remembering, old country connections
Giving rise to many traditions, eventually blues, jazz, rock, roll and rap
First including shouts, hollers, work songs, fife and drums, and spirituals
Soon though I was eyed suspiciously, regarded as dangerous
Inspiring identity, rebellion fomenting, taken by Reverend Clark
on behalf of a man named Sloane, for his collection
My provenance hidden, shrouded in mystery, supposedly of Amerindian ancestry
Only later did curators realise my African American object status
Now museum goers listen in, to my dramatic narratives, my skins of flexibility
not adhering to a singular history, revelling in my
rubato rhythms, inclined ears exalt

Dandelion Diaspora

Proud nations given alien status
Stateless seed dispersal
The dandelion clock
Ticks, tocks and makes a wish

Blown from West Africa's shores
To the auction block
To plantations of tobacco and cotton picking
Fingers snap and find New World rhythms
In shock, millions of magical florets,
Lost
Descend then globe trot

Golden Akan crowns bend down, disintegrate
Into silver tufted afro puffs
Grown grey-weary with time-fate
Clocks, blowballs, ticking timebombs

Awaiting

Glorious explosion, regenerate
Puffed parachutes land
Around a pappus vortex ring of smoke
Enriching drab projects, housing estates
Sewing new treasured seeds
Rapid colonisation of disturbed soils

Continuity of bright silky kente tapestry
Once stripped, re-stitched
Coast to coast, across
Connecting Atlantic rifts
Once sailed by slave ships

Ticks, tocks and makes a wish
The dandelion clock
Stated seed dispersal
Alien status creates proud nations

Slave to the Rhythm

Collusion, illusion, colonial fantasy
Speak Fante, Ashanti,
Brit, Dane and Dutch
Portuguese fortresses
Of slaughtered sons and daughters
Tower above
Pillaging through inland villages, they trudge
To the edge of humanity
Through the door of no return

Forgotten//Lost
Sons and Daughters
Incarcerated tortures and traumas
Incinerated fortunes
Fortified slaughter

Piled up commodities
Burnished stacks of Gold
On a Coast of latticed limbs
Betrayed by the half dead
Wriggle of toes
Trickle of urine from above
On sickly faecal floors

Tribal flags
Unfurled
Scars run deep
On the ocean floored
Corpses hooked, lined
Sunk and moored
Forgotten//Lost
Sons and Daughters

Incarcerated tortures and traumas
Incinerated fortunes
Fortified slaughter

Over dungeons
Others coast on golden stools
In a church on the upper castle

Field negro, house negro
Akwaabas
Sold
Put on a plinth
By men on ivory pedestals
Like butcher's mince
Scales of fortune
Slide and slip
The cat o'nine tails
Cracks
Flesh under the Master's whip

Forgotten//Lost
Sons and Daughters
Incarcerated tortures and traumas
Incinerated fortunes
Fortified slaughter
Lost tongues and voices

My Golden Coast

Part One

As a child I flexed my mother's tongue
Asante Twi,
On dusty laterite compound steps
Fading Portuguese facades and colonial schemes
An Empire of broken dreams

Ghana,
What do you mean to me?
What do you owe to me?

A romanticised vision convinced me
Of a royal return Roots and all
An answer to Haley's clarion call

Fufu pounds,
Plantain fries
Bringing contented sighs as family abounds

In '77 cold English skies
Froze hitherto our sun-drenched African lives
Sounds and memories slowly evaded
Sanguine hopes of another me shaded
'What is Ghana like?' I quizzed my mother
In a Bedfordshire tongue
In a market town garden was I led up the path
Kept in the dark?

Part Two

I cried tears for this faraway treasured land
My Gethsamene awaited
The dreams would not subside

I pictured a warm embrace and *Akwaaba*
Or was this an ill-fitting fiction?
Set up against the backdrop of Thatcher's theatrical Britain
Riots and miners' strikes
What is your fate when two cultures collide?
Was I to become a vultured victim?

Touch-down to reality in the 1990's,
Surprise
Landing upon Ghanaian soil
A blanket of warmth embroils
That first African night the talking drumbeats pound
Undulating tribal voices reverberate, confound
New sounds envelop
So many blacks:
Red black, blackcurrant black, plum black, blueberry black
greet the whites of my eyes.

On a new continuum of colour I am seen as *Obroni*
A white in their lives
Disoriented in a dark room of negative perception

In Britain I am black
In Ghana I am white
The realisation of the Middle way is born,
Shades of grey unhinge my door

Ordinary Hybrid Bliss

Amidst maisonette curtained streets
Flanking the park in NW6
Chewing on mundane realities
Rice, peas, roast beef and chapattis
White Teeth chatter convivially
In this corner of the metropolis
Ordinary hybrid bliss

Racial difference reduced to oblivion

Concrete sciences set in mind stone
Discriminating simplification
Histories, objects, places and times
Mutants, foreigners, roles assigned
Classed as confusing, destructive objects
Fabricated into fictional reality

In the Houses of Khan and Adebisi
Two up two down
Imaginative geography vanishes
Jamaican-Yoruba-Pakistani neighbours
Everyday mundane relations
Upstairs Downstairs Hybrid Nation
Wed in the matrimony of exotic estrangement
White Teeth chatter convivially
In this corner of the metropolis
Ordinary hybrid bliss

Racial difference reduced to oblivion

We design in our mind's eye
Familiar spaces: yours and mine; ours and theirs

Arbitrary designs, (un)familiar places
Imaginative geographies, boundaries established in minds
Our land/barbarian land binaries
Territory and mentality demarcated negative identities

Yousef and Ibrahim stutter through Bismillah
Winsome and Habiba discuss diets of how to get thinner
White Teeth chatter convivially
In this corner of the metropolis
Ordinary hybrid bliss

Racial difference reduced to oblivion

The poetics of space
Intimacies, secrecy and security
Corners, corridors, cellar rooms
Objective space reduced to imaginative value
Emotional areas made rational
By poetic process, vacant anonymous reaches
Distance converted into meaning

Oluwale and Irshad bemoan their sons'
poor performance at madrassa
White Teeth chatter convivially
In this corner of the metropolis
Ordinary hybrid bliss

Racial difference reduced to oblivion

Imaginative geography and history
Intensifying sense of self
Dramatizing distance and difference
by what is close and far away
Represents, animates, creates
otherwise silent and dangerous space
Beyond familiar boundaries

Ibrahim and Yousef listen to beats
of spontaneous and ordinary hybridity
plugged into their headphones
Technologically trebled and based in this city
White Teeth chatter convivially
In this corner of the metropolis
Ordinary hybrid bliss

Racial difference reduced to oblivion

Intersectional identities, solidarity
Class, gender, sex and faith
rendering race unthinkable
Beyond skin invisible

White Teeth chatter convivially
In this corner of the metropolis
Ordinary hybrid bliss
Racial difference reduced to oblivion

Rich—Genetic Commonwealth

'You gotta get outta here'
Tried to make me a stranger—'outsider *hear!*'
Victim of another's fear,
Victim of another's sphere?

My soul can't be controlled
Can't pigeon-hole a racing pigeon,
In the smoke I signal I'm an indigenous survivor,
Messenger with bottle,
Brimming full with lexical reflexes, psyche vexed,

Striver, alpine climber,
Attitude

High

On altitude

You gotta stack of words for me.
But Paki don't suffice,
Nigger,
That don't figure.
Not a mongrel but a thorough
Bred with stronger genes when mixed
Simply complex with compound interest
No more of Gobineau's tricks:
Genetics
Not eugenics

Consternation—to race haters
Hate orators play against miscegenation
Pseudo-scientific stiflers of creation 0

Ciphered by Afro-futurism
Humans won!
Job's been done

Confusion—cystic fibrosis can't cope with us,
Under a gavel sickle cell
                    sell is ...
Sold ... to the man with genetic wealth,

A healthy balance

Bank on us.

Kpanlogo—Rewriting History

I scrawled *Breakdance* in thin pink ink
Capital B stood tall
next to letters joined in deference, small
Felt, tipped, penned memory indelibly inked
Its velvet nib pressed rough
resisting antelope skin
Stretched by elephant tusks
hammered in the barrel of the drum
rim fastening with overlapping, diagonal
wild cat's cradle decorations
An eighties B-boy in Leighton
Buzzard surrounded by eagle mysteries
Buddha in suburbia
desperately trying to rewrite history

Mum brought back various gifts
from her visit to mourn Nana Yaa's passing:
a carved crocodile, a talking drum for Michael
and this kpanlogo
Precious cargo, chest of treasure
a long lost home on a golden Ga coast
Landing in my hands a barrel
Bounty for a ghost pirate, keg of rum
from faraway travels and troubles
Humble drum housing unknown tones, qualities
My mum told me in Twi, it was called *tswreshi*
In the fifties, to echo independence,
it was renamed kpanlogo

Thanking her, I caressed it tenderly,
Its smooth African cedar, like a potter at a wheel
Weighing up its *tweneboa* master crafted construction

timber of medium density
Later, I graffitied on its skin, secretly
to give it some meaning, to rewrite history

Odondo Talking

Umbilical chords of tension sing

I have another confession I must mention
We cut the umbilical cords
Tension to our motherland
Second generation, relaxing,
Easing our connections,
as we loosened the sinewy heartstrings
in a semi-det in Bedfordshire
forever indebted to the message:
to the balance books
of assimilation at all costs

We severed the dark red threads
of leather, cagily, that encased
Michael's drum, from Ghana
another present from our mum
Denuded it, further revealing
Its hourglass figuring
Refashioned history
we made, bespoke bracelets
costume jewellery, pure tom-tom foolery

Lost for words we couldn't hear in Twi
It remained an unheard mystery
Melodious notes on bitonal Akan language scale
Differently inflected complex messages
Carrying soundwaves, travelling across villages
Herald of special occasions
calls to arms, addressing subject nations,
warning attacks and ceremony
Single words translated into contextual phrases
Passed on stick to palm by courtly griot sages
Performing on a stage, hereditary lineage tuition

Intuitions, connecting DNA double helix
c(h)ords of genetic muscle memory flexed
oral literature, ritualised performances,
drums and scores forming proverbs,
panegyrics, historical epics, dirges and poems

Achieved by varying tension
On opposing drumheads in cord connection
Held between drummer's arms and ribs
Rhythm, volume, pitch, regulated during a single beat
hit with accompanying free hand,
dampening, producing rubbery textures,
warbling wah-wah pedalled sounds
Whole phrase humming like humans
Matching complex heavy Kwahu language

Language and literature, curved sticks
wands, magical tricks on the edge of drum lips
secret, griot history of Ashanti Kings

Wake Up Call

'Post' racial racisms proliferate at the wake
Maggots burrow and suck the marrow
Of the bony body, stiff, upper lipped, quivering
Where supposedly race has died
Rigor Mortis
Rigorous post-mortem sets in

We sit in its wake, denying the corpse
Unvoiced
Brutalized by the ghost—invisible institutions
Structured denial, structures of the mind
Post-mortem staining
Livor Mortis blue, veins deoxygenated, bruised
Trodden down, choked by the boys in the same hue
And cry the threats
Quelled, securitized
surveillance capital capturing insurgents
by militarized law forcers
caught on the grainy black and white reality CCTV
Animalized in Gazan strip search malls,
Mauled beside Ferguson's suburban stores
Contained in a wooden box, bodies bagged
Body's race declassified in the state morgue
A race to legally deny
Neo-liberal accountability privatised
Outbreaks, viralities, skirmishes informalized
Penetrating gated communities and nations

Murmurs on the 'Make Britain Great Again' News
Channelling emotional narratives
Irrational unevidenced indignation
Speakers spit and hiss poisonous noises

Surround soundbites of disavowal
Anti-Woke Culture Wars waged against a home front truth
National Service rings in ears, called to action
Death knells toll, entrenched
Hollow sounds in post-truth age battles
History rewritten, weaponised,
Perpetrators victimised

Unearthed historical facts, developments arrested; held hostage
by eulogized mythologies, emotional narratives
Covered up, unevidenced indignation,
Electronic pages rewritten and shared from ivory towers,
White Houses, Parliaments of snowy owls defecating, disseminating
Bubo scandiacus, scandalous excretions
Fake acidic news, dropping ammonia pellet bombs of undigested truths
From rooves, whilst beneath them
the undocumented polish whitewashed glass ceilings
Ethnic cleansing, ethical cleaning

Wiping down the blood splattered walls
Entranced halls of un*stately* homes, historic edifices
Systems, structures built on the foundations
Of a disappearing, Bermudian triangle of transatlantic slavery
Baroque gold gilded framed portraits
Vanishing points of reference, reverence

Country houses for those seeking asylum
Amputees immobilised, shell-shocked cultured
Victims, entrenched survivors of colonial empires
Sit then sleep in a post-Brexit divided, ruled,
Above the eye, identity clings to soils
Ploughed embattled furrowed brows
Born and raised rich, dormant garden beds of privilege
Signalling denial

Hedgerow colonial countryside, gangrene unpleasant land
Suffering the blight of a Black Plague, bubonic, ruins
The bucolic myth of Merrie England reimagined
Rebuilding Hadrian's Walls, Fortress Britannia barricaded
Arcadia manipulated with Capability the Browns and Blacks and Others
Banished from the Middle of English villages
Subjects to anthroporacial fertilisation,
pesticides and sterilisation, vanish

In a court of disapproval, donned, undone, unacademic:
A squad of climate scientists and historians of Empire
Lined up and sentenced by jesters: jingoistic juries jeering
Cheered on by structures of denial and disapproval
Denounced unpatriotic leftie liars.

Rigorous post-mortem sets in
Rigor Mortis
Where supposedly race has died
On the bony body, stiff, upper lipped, quivering
Maggots burrow and suck the marrow
'Post' racial racisms proliferate at the wake.

SONG

(mind)

Songs of Grime

George Herbert and William Blake sang poems in drawing rooms
Now we spit lyrics of innocence and experience in inner-city bedsits

with DIY mixing equipment spinning the helms, turning the tables
in pirate radio ships stationed on the top of tower blocks

From the galop and Viennese Waltz to the dubstep and skank
In ancient Greece winning poets were crowned with wreathes

Laurels and foolhardy grime MCs battle over plinths for block
supremacy and postcode stakes, Stone Island statues dressed

with Fred Perry Roadman Supreme on the North Face
Greensleeves sampled whilst the green leaves sacred to Apollo

Gods of Poetry go toe to toe. A Rocky Horrorshow of mercing and shanking
Akala translates Shakespeare sonnets into ghetto phonics

A Merchant of Vengeance putting penance and microphone to paper
Stair-welled screw-faced revenge Measure for Measure

Opening caskets of lexical treasure
Melodious poems of praise, elegiac mourning and memory

Liverpool *Eight* Names

Liverpool 8 names, playing out racist games
in a stadium of hate, under the floodlights
that lost their *shine*, instantly dimmed dark
A Polaroid faded light over time, photoshopped, gentrified
Gladiators deflecting heat with thick skinned shields
radiating from chariots of fire
whether in Anfield or Goodison Park
modern colosseums feeding Africans to lions
Puzzle People torn and left to pick up the pieces

Negro in the forties, *Mixed Race* sixties *Shines*
Coloured a *half-caste* in the nineteen seventies
Afro-Caribbean eighties status, Ethnic Minority nineties
Ticking a box, somewhere on a millennium
Ethnic Monitoring Form penned stateless

The sixties shines darkened by Scouse black humour
Half cast aside, half apart from Fathers without Mersey phrasebooks
who clung to the last pages of yellowing institutions:
The Federation, The Crew Club, The Sierra Leone,
The Nigerian, The Yoruba, The Ethiopian, The Ibo
Dreaming of setting sail on fresh zephyrs to Africa again
No reason why their sons and daughters could not assimilate
Docked from slavery, colonialism, poverty and wars
Trying to shield their children from racial tortures

Born in Liverpool lonely, home not a free town Sierra Leone
Here to stay but isolated as a *Yellow Man*, *Half Breed*, *Red*
Confronted in streets head-to-head, considered English
by their Fathers, born in the middle of an ocean, lost
in a Bermudian triangle of transatlantic slavery
Feet in all camps: African language, Liverpudlian culture

Carrying on a revolt, brave, continuing lineage of diaspora slaves
Be it in Massa's plantation/ targets of the KKK/ rioters in Watts
Apartheid Soweto home townships/ Ashanti warrior war fields
Maroons in Jamaican mountains/ Mau Mau resisting
Painting Washington BLM yellow/ part of a proud Nation

Games of classification, nominated nomenclature
Pencilling fifty shades of degra(y)dation
Shards of glass pressed into hearts deflating
Darkie, glasses worn to avoid the experience of *Shines*
Lenses framing innocence 'No 'arm was ever meant, soft lad.'

'You'll Never Walk Alone' the chant
for Barnes bananas thrown and monkey groans apart
Bananas split, both sides in laughter
Aping civilisation terraces of institutionalised racism
Cheered on in the stadium of hate, Jekyll and Hyde
Whilst they applaud the Caucasian scorers
without pause or falter, haitus from terrace torture
Walking through a storm, head held high, unafraid of dark

Wandering across from Red to Blue
Through an A–Z maze of slaver street names
past Penny Lane, it drops, James Penny
Strawberry Fields of blood run bittersweet
Wrapped in cotton wool Protectionism at all costs
to stem against the Union flow, the *Oreto* leaves, in secrecy,
Enrica renamed *CSS Alabama*, supporting Confederacy
Capturing, burning and sinking sixty-five merchant ships

Arriving at Everton's proposed new home
Bramley Moore's Docksite Stadium to Slavery
Slaveowner and merchant of Brazilians
Complicit in the violence of middle passage misery
Financing clandestine voyages, lucrative deliveries
Who spoke out against an Act in Parliament

against British naval ships inspecting for enslaved cargoes
Receiving Pedro II's Order of the Rose

Liverpool 8 names, playing out racist games
in a stadium of hate, under the floodlights
that lost their *shine*, instantly dimmed dark
A Polaroid faded light over time, photoshopped, gentrified
Gladiators deflecting heat with thick skinned shields
radiating from chariots of fire
whether in Anfield or Goodison Park
modern colosseums feeding Africans to lions
Puzzle People torn and left to pick up the pieces

Negro in the forties, *Mixed Race* sixties *Shines*
Coloured a *half-caste* in the nineteen seventies
Afro-Caribbean eighties status, Ethnic Minority nineties
Ticking a box, somewhere on a millennium
Ethnic Monitoring Form cutting costs

Carrying on a revolt, brave, continuing lineage of diaspora slaves
Be it in Massa's plantation/ targets of the KKK/ rioters in Watts
Apartheid Soweto home townships/ Ashanti warrior war fields
Maroons in Jamaican mountains/ Mau Mau resisting
Painting Washington BLM yellow/ part of a proud Nation
Walk on, walk on with hope in our hearts
At the end of the storm there's a rainbow
and a sweet golden song of calypso
We will never walk alone. This is our home.

The Writing on the Wall

'Wogs out' the graffiti sprayed
In those Bedfordshire days
That led me to question
With what affection
was my sort held?

Signed 'NF' in marker pen iridescence
On pallid South Beds Council urinals
Indecencies scrawled indelibly
On my mind
That led me to question
With what affection
was my sort held?

The shards of corner shop glass
Thwarted our fragile path
To post-racial harmony
We lived in the Dark decades
Ages
Of ignorance and violence
Was it my problem?
That the chant was sung:
'Pakis outnumbered 10 to 1'
That led me to question
With what affection
was my sort held?

In morbid expectation
I awaited black History pages
Of dehumanised victims

Beads of perspiration created
A red glow of knowing tinged my skin
As I uncomfortably listened in
To narratives
Of the passive recipients of slavery
Tragedies with no heroes
That led me to question
With what affection
was my sort held?

In contemplation
Was it your intention?
For me to assent to
Condescending classifications
And ideas of Nation?

Racism was never mentioned
In those Bedfordshire days

Ghana Songs of Praise

Dad grew vegetables,
behind a pebble-dashed semi-det
[a hyphenated arrangement]
in the next-door neighbours' gardens,
elderly widows, named Betty and Margaret
[Margaret was a Cockney Huguenot;
Betty a Leighton Buzzard local]
Hungry for escape,
with a giant fork, in his hand

He grew mostly Maris Pipers,
swedes, carrots and parsnips,
runner beans on bamboo, wig wams
Calloused hands of sandpaper
from the soil and spade

We pulled up their ripe roots,
plugs from the sink
We shook off clinging earth
like dogs after a bath

Dad wrote sermons,
in the conservatory,
where he marked essays
and graded them, in red pen
Often, he travelled, up and down arpeggios,
scaling memories, peacefully
overlapping dovetailed dreams,
playing hymns,
from Ghana Songs of Praise
Dad played the piano
beside the table tennis table

folded up, like a handkerchief,
its edges covered in adinkra
shining black on undyed cloth,

Next to his desk sat the carved tusks
of an elephant, curved top, varnished above,
carrying prayer books and papers

Dad wore kente ties and batakaris
that billowed on his lean frame
He missed Ghana, more than my mum

Kamikaze Kwahu Taxi

In Nyame we trust
Kamikaze taxi held by rust
Heading hell for leather, soles
departing the clutch, shifting our gear
hopefully for heaven, sandal on pedal,
up the Kwahu escarpment
We leave Nkawkaw's red,
laterite soil for dust
Where I was born Kwabena
on a Tuesday,

We alight this yellow-blue time machine
Wheels spin like a scene fast and furiously
Decorated bullet hole perforations,
we notice there is only one door,
the other must have corroded
road reversing through holy floor
We climb like a rollercoaster
rising vertical before, helter-
skelter turns on the mountain

Halfway up, we reach Atibie, green foliage,
serene, where my brother Kwadwo was raised,
born on a Monday,
The air thins yet thickens with pregnant
pausing thoughts unspoken
Dad and I smile with exhilaration
The driver nods at our patience
Tooting his horn repeatedly:
twenty-one salutes of joy
My mum sighs in exasperation
For her birth nation

Just like an obroni been-to
travelling with abrofo family
when she was on the tro tro only last week
exploding with fuming frustration,
as we waited for the driver's mate
to load up at Cape Coast, after a trip to Elmina,
you should have seen her
but that's another story for later
I think about telling when we sharpen a corner,
round a bend

We continue our ascent, circling escarpment
Vultures on a flight path
In passing we pray for a lorry lying prostrate
that had vomited its timber
logs spilled lining the road
a signal of danger

Up as far as Obomeng
we pause, for a funeral procession
the seventh day of celebrations
possession of ancestors, joining
the dead on their journey, singing,
accompanied by dancing and drumming

Observed on a Saturday, deceased laid in state
adorned with gold jewellery
thousands flowing red and black robes
Blackcurrant ants from a former British colony
pallbearing a sun varnished caramel leaf
its golden handles curled by light

We disembark in Obo,
where my mum was born,
on a Thursday, Yaa
High in the clouds, we laugh in relief

We had climbed the escarpment
Gye Nyame
Praise omniscient Sky God Onyankopɔn
We had reached heaven
in a kamikaze taxi

Identity Parade

Lootin' and robbin' hoodies in a knottingham concrete forest
Low slung denim worn, with African genes
So the stereotyped slights go
Tabloid headlines tattoo 'Black on Black Gun Grime'
Serenaded by sirens and alarm
Fear flutters the broad-sheeted bubble of Lenton Boulevard
Accidentally veering way of Radford into the mystery of Hyson Green

A sophomore student of anthropology and archaeology
Digs located in Johnson Road
Worn down by the dress code of Lace Market clubbing clothes
Ralph Lauren polo; Paul Smith fresh from the wardrobe

From the Gold Coast, young, Ghanaian and proud,
Brought up since '77 in a Bedfordshire market town,
Rounding the corner, diasporas lost and found

In '97 reinvented
Massively Attacked by trip hop
At the Marcus Garvey Centre
Skylarkin' and skankin' to Horace Andy
Warm Tennent's Super in hand
Weaving from disaster

On my way home I heard a Soca sound
Entering a West Indian shebeen
Red Stripe served over a formica screen
Dominoes slap on tables turned
Reggae, ska and rocksteady served by the DJ

On a turntable platter

From Lenton, along Radford Road
Third year explorations further afield
As far as the Trent pub scene's Arboretum
Where I was greeted as an easy picking
A bouncer suggested I attend identity parade
Cash registered by a certain shade
Funds to supplement my studies in drinking
In Hyson Green police station, what was I thinking?

Lined up, ready and free to be picked
Afropean faces nasalise East Midlands patois
Sending panic to my Home Counties ear
Fear ripened in my plummy mouth
Vowel movements muted a difference I dared not pronounce
I stood with my kin from the other side of the city

Lamb Roast

Kiwi Chris lit the stove by matchstick
A two pack from Londis for less than a quid
Sacrificed for us to savour, the slow
Luscious lamb roast
Slow cooking mindfulness
Cooked at the zenith of suburbia
Sitting sweet in its juices
Served with West Hampstead
Garden salad suburb addressing
In matrimony with mashed potato
Scooped onto faux bone china
'Good feed eh?'
Understated New Zealand roast.

Sicily

Limoncello on lips
Lemon ice granita
Sticky on your finger, tips
Frozen espresso at the beach
In dainty plastic cups
Rectangular pizza cut
Incisions, into slices with scissors
Aperitifs taken on marbled benches
Walnuts are shelled
Old friends sit outside
Greco-Roman facades
Sand-stoned labyrinths
Narrow streets
Car horn choruses

Loved Up

A love rhyme
We drank the reddest wine
Berries bled in merriment
Played Scrabble in her bed
Listening to Nick Cave's
Haunting hymns and verses
Played out in our heads
Sheltered from inner city climes
Shuddered as the Bakerloo line trains
Vibrated in mesmerising time
A love rhyme

Victorian Portal

At the brick red Victorian door, Harvist Road
next to the Tube Station
Guarded, by the dark iron Gothic lion,
doorknocker snarling, I stand at the basement flat
I lift its jaw wide open, pausing
pulling at the sinews of my heartstrings
Set, frozen aspic hope
in the frosty liminal morning
on the boundary of the Corporation park
Legs jellied anticipation, body mind in syncopation,
a snow globe left unshaken stirring silence
Shuddering in time with the Bakerloo Line
trains of thoughts, caught in the ghostly
opening and closing of underground doors

Suspended service of adrenaline injection
Passenger, patient awaiting ejection from a tubed chamber
of yet to be known, secret destination
Life's poison or elixir, quick or dead at my lips, not yet sipped
Fingertips quivering, holding the tablet, not yet swallowed
Philosopher's stone cold sober tinged hangover

We'd met the night before, hit it off
At the gastro pub we'd sat
in the snug, smug selves satisfied we'd met
Manic conversation lubricated by libation
We'd thanked God for destiny, we'd laughed a lot

Now I turned my back, uncertain of re-entry
Number 48, verdigris accumulating
Doorway degrees of separation
Blue-green eyed, lion roar, jealously regarding me

Numerology counted, it was meant to be
My childhood addressed, inverted 84,
it had passed the fateful test
Hovering at the door, should I knock or let it rest?

I stood, confused,
muddled and muggled
Like Harry Potter at a Platform,
nine and three-quarters
uncertain, unsure
hesitating
at a portal

Latvian Lines in the Snow

The trumpeter blows in blankets of snow
Cold, crisp wintry images
Our brains in shock froze
Gold glistens and shines incongruent against white
A Baltic feast for our eyes in which to delight

Tourists searching for familiar sights
Arrive aghast amidst shelves and boulders of ice
A boy scrambles up crunching white rubble
Unsure footing causes him to trip
and stumble

Later I twitch behind my hotel window's iron curtain
Snowflakes fall fluffily, pregnant potential on pause
On the granite of unwelcoming steps
A man with two shovels scrapes at crystalline depths

Chil(l)dren drag the heels of their sledges to school
Satchels screwed to their backs
In the shadows of Soviet flats, cemented Eastern housing b-l-o-c-s

Onto a whirring tram with wooden floors
Passengers in fur coats fox trot on board
The lonely tinkle signals our stop

Upon disembarkation
Our pace quickens
Syncopated footstep rhythms
Stacca-toed inhalations of icy air
Awkward anticipation of cold local stares
With reassurance we follow the sound of MTV
Spilling out from an Old Town Rigan cobbled corner

To a musical bar named Klondike in neon

It sparkles with promise before us
Forming a tawdry noisy chorus:
Fruit machines pirouette and glint
Subdued behind windows of heavy tint

We self-consciously tiptoe in
Down
Down Down
Dark steps to a
Subterranean counter

Pear ciders in hand we loiter
A young man's eyes now fix on my face
In deliberation and worrying cadence,
He intones, 'May ... I ... take your phot ... o?'
In accented Lativian English

Nervously my eyes avert to the floor
He elaborates
'You see I haven't seen a *black* man before.'

I look up, relieved at this positive attention
In the corner of my eye I decline to mention
The ironic hues of hip hop performers
On the music video behind us,
from a distance, regarded as normal

Evening Class

Radical: about the inherent roots of an issue
Anthropology: the study of what it means to be human

The professor lectures in a tatty leather waistcoat, worn
in a room with wallpaper peeling, torn,
on myths and fables, rubbing his temples of doom
in concentration, pacing the room
like the Crystal Maze presenter
He addresses his comrades, crossing Rubicon confusion
Parting a red sea of tape, academic obstruction, swimming
against the current, against Neo-Darwinian
selfish genetics

Whilst primordial soup is poured,
food for our thoughts
in an unglamorous Camden kitchen,
a Tuesday evening ritual,
ladled for a two-pound fifty contribution
sitting in chipped bowls wonky on trestle tables
at Saint Martin's Community Centre

Dialectical moves, a shiny armoured Knight, in leather
Chris-crossing a kinship chequerboarded flooring,
checkmating academic opposition, total knockouts
Debunking Levi Straussian savage minds, jousting
Mythologiques, charging at Chomsky, providing
insights into a human revolution
menstrual sex strikes

A Tuesday moonlit talk of lunar phases,
The Walilak Sisters and menstruation,
Ochred crayon cross-hatchings carbon dated

Prehistoric images in Blombos Caves, symbolic
illumination, a social revolution makes echo
in mythic narratives, ritual traditions,
still heard in reverberation, around our globe
Symbolic cultural emergence from a rift in a valley
An African DNA garden of Eden
mitochondrial Eve cradling, encephalisation, civilisation
heads and tongues spinning, larynxes dropping
with human language, making space for tongue movement,
speech production full throttle no glottal stops,
vocal tract acrobatics, spectacular oral gymnastics
vaulted roofs render religion and culture,
on palates palatial, emerging in a revolution
not gradual Darwinian evolution
The lecturer lures his audience
fishing for challenges,
disagreement and counter-examples
Looks at them sternly, curiosity above bi-focals
Making foreplay, teasing, exploding illusions of nuclear families
Familiarities, patriarchal nods, winks
matrilineal systems restoration and particle paternity

Often his friends, interdisciplinary experts,
wander in to seated ovations
Sharing their latest hypotheses, crusty bread
and a soupcon of their latest discoveries
Guests in lectures wax lyrically
Algis wades in with his aquatic ape theory,
Lionel Sims watches on,
adjusting his clock of lunar synchronicity,
Camilla powers simultaneously with a sex strike thesis
while the iron ladle in the soup is still hot,
Evening class; human revolution

Lounge Lizard

Attracted to the pull of Mullumbimby baize
Stretched out hinterland hills fill
A kaleidoscope of backgrounds amidst eucalypt purple haze

We drive past the Council building
Bureaucracy palmed off by its trees
Down Station Street as two travellers
Swig bottles of beer and wash their faces
In the morning sun

Happily absolving themselves of the nine to five grit and grind
At the municipal fountain
Rush hour in Mullumbimby

GPS sends us to a darkened oasis sheltering from swelter
In the sand pit in its corner sits a sweaty cherub
Shifting sands in diapers in own his leisurely time

We enter under the bowed bough of an ancient gum
A Shinto gateway
Shuffling in, met by bone china chinks of pleasure
Rubber tyred chairs lounge on the floor
Bright Mexican Day of the Dead flags quiver in breeze

Sweet bitter coffee roasts in our noses
And parches our throats
As I order and await my delivery
I walk around a circular raised deck in mahogany
Its wooden slats like the keys of a piano

In the shade of the deck between two Vittoria coffee stands
Do my eyes deceive me?

A hipster bearded dragon
Squatting on its forearms
Lounging on its haunches
Pulsating subtly to the slow dubbed beat
Od Reggae Plastique

Its mascara runs from its eye
Down its triangular head
Crowned by rows of thorns
Under its chin rows of spikes puff up into a beard
Changing colour from green to khaki, the lizard broods
In reflective mood, tapping its fingers on the keyboard
Scales upon scales

DREAM

(heart)

Ochre-Masked Avatars

Ochre-masked avatar, incarnation of human symbolism
Bodily manifestation of human deity
Ochre daubed as blood mask

Ochre-masked avatar, human revolution of art
Song, ritual and dance
Masking confusion
Female evolution, withholding fertility

Ochre-masked avatar, concealed ovulation
Loss of oestrus, depriving impregnation
Reproductive cycle synchrony
Birth of symbolic culture

Ochre-masked avatar, painting up blood red
For evolutionary effect
Increasing male investment
Encephalization

Ochre-masked avatar, ritual, myth, culture
Female invention for
Offspring investment
Simultaneous sex strikes

Raffles

The cloud of colonial aftershocks hang over
Seismic shifts in waves, washed down and out

Welcome pink drinks served in haste
Singapore slingshots down planes
Engulfed Cosmopolitan flames
Flying too close to the orange
Peeling Rising Sun, kamikaze
Flaming fuselage oils singe
Acidic citrus skins plummeting

Landlocked promises, shelled in shock
Peanut husks discarded on hardwood
Floored empires set in horizon dusk
Ground into the dust
Drunk wounded war prisoners
Decline into wicker chairs absorbing shock
Lost in heady cocktail, covered faded umbrella
Glace cherry civilisation

Sweet bitterness, loss of flavour
Guests dance, one final waltz to savour

Steel Pulse

Feel its steel pulse
Iron racehorse
Opening its steely jaws
Carrying warriors black bareback
Through red canals
Veins in the heartland
Rivers foaming, frothing blood source

There's a revolution in Handsworth
Feel its steel pulse
Galvanising urban black youth
The Black Country defiant
Afros matting and hardening resistance
to stem the rivers red compliance

Kids growing locks of consciousness
Next to canals of blood
Feel its steel pulse
Haile Selassie badges pinned
tams worn on crowns in honour
Lions of Judah join Jack's Union
Young dreads maturing, forming
Grand conga Unions
inseparably rooted

Born in a Black Country
Smethwick, Griffiths, Powell,
Babylon System of victimisation
Feel its steel pulse
Stopped and searched, eye suspiciously
Cold metal stainless ring
Or*biting* my wrists,

Pinching my handcuffed skin
Bullring piercing

Questioning the Establishment
Rhetorical reggae, jazz fused punk
Answers back
Bringing steel pans from Trinidad
Percussion from rubbish
Feel its steel pulse
Play influential rhythms
From humble beginnings
Sons of poor West Indians
with comical monikers:
Grizzly, Phonson, Stepper and Bumbo

Rocksteady against racism
They silence Clapton's hypocritical bigotry
and anti-immigrant rants in '76
Vowing allegiance with Powell
Fear of a Black Country
Keep the British White
Yet he covered 'I Shot the Sheriff'
Feel its steel pulse
Time for self-defence

Nyah Love music, hate racism
Communicating to urban black youth
and white subterranean punks
Messengers with soothing music
Lullabies sung to the womb of Mother Africa
Performing a class critique on stage
Clothed as an eighteenth-century footman
Feel its steel pulse
bowler hat, cassock and tails
representing feudal regalia

Stacking a sound system of black boxers
Against a System stacked against them
Shutting down, knocking out the Klu Klux Klan
Feel the electrical steel pulse
Sparking a Handsworth Revolution
Steady melodic flow of electrons
Politically charged
Kings of Ethiopia, Lions of Judah
Feel its steel pulse
Praising His Imperial Majesty Haile Selassie
Regal racial philosophy of love
Promulgating against African Holocaust
Unearthing hidden mysteries,
reclamation of a stolen legacy
Sharp sociological tools
to look upon the culture of ancestors
Formation of a complex, true identity

Iron racehorse escaping wooden gates of Troy
Opening its steely jaws
Ridden by warriors, feel its steel pulsating
Expanding through its shiny covering
Fetlocks on sodden ground—
Hinged, allowing flexion and extension
Manes flow in the lightening flash of dreadlocks
brown velvet skin,
hurdling, steeplechasing red frothing puddles
jumps surmounting, Feel its steel pulse

Comfort Food

As Comfort cooks on gas, often she inhales
Akan aphorisms, proverbs that she knew
Remembering the sweetness of plantain
Stirring memories in her palm, nut stew
Fermenting dreams, unravelling kenkey's
protective casing, from a ma(i)ze of truth
The husks shedded of former youth and health
Never can she be parted from her wealth

Once pounding fufu in a giant mortar
Cassava struck in time by wooden pestle
Asante villager, amazing daughter
Sitting atop a golden stool of treasure
A-head carrying bucket, brimming water
Quickened steps ignoring blazing weather
Running, escaping heavy escarpment air
Exhaling past, present and future prayers

Keep the Aspidistra Flying

Venus flies trapped by
stiff upper lips
in the middle-class distance
Keep the aspidistra flying

Double glazed over dreams
waft briefly
boxed behind
privet hedged hysteria
They kept the aspidistra flying

Generations of poisoned ivy cling
drowned out
by waterfalls of wisteria
Keep the aspidistra flying

Rock garden battlement
Council house castles
Yellow smoke screened curtains
Lace peri-urban view
They kept the aspidistra flying

Satellite citadels of dishes
BSky B is the limit
Picking up the wrong signals
of C list celebrity indiscretions
Keep the aspidistra flying

Guarded gates sentried
Picket white fences
Meditated and mediated
by Bhuddas of Suburbia

supplanting rows of gnomes
Cabbages and lettuce cower
They kept the aspidistra flying

Led up the crazy paving
to coping stone walls
and pebble-dashed hopes
Keep the aspidistra flying

Musical ringtones greet you
at the resin Roman columns
Lions cast in plastic Garden centred surgery
Moulded to the floor
We keep the aspidistra flying

Blossom

Ephemeral pink pleasure
Lightly glowing, lightening lives,
Lined under Odawaran sakura skies,
One thousand cherry trees burgeon in breeze
One thousand springing dreams

Office workers lay fruitfully
Under Ueno Park blossom reverie,
Lightly petals blow
Sowing seeds of spring

Sake scented skies darken
Illuminated by blushed bulbs on high,

Night-time excited white-pink

Cracks

If you're not careful, you'll disappear through the cracks
Waxed lyrically the clipped Cockney estate agent chap,
clad in Barbour topped with flat cap,
Clive, bright eyed barrow boy brimming expectantly wide
Prospecting at rents on the Rise

Middle manager's self-conscious shoes
shined and smiling
Full of ringtones and rent-books
He reached for his lighter, my false hopes igniting
Mimed Hackneyed phrases and friendly right hooks
Clive tap-danced along his Manor's granny flats and nooks,

Laying real estate landmines,
Hooked on leasing boxrooms and bedsits
In subdivided and ruled Zone 3's Kensal Greenery

Polluted by a Harrowed, treeless trunk Road
With no ATM branches or public amenities,
Filthy deposits litter the path
Shops boarded in the dark, stock-taken by vagrants
Clutching Special Brew cans in fingerless gloved hands

Pot-holes and crack houses back to back
Bohemian shabby chic of Ladbroke Grove bo(ar)ders

Listen out for Mr B-Line in 14 B(eats)
Abandons his forklift at the end of the night's shift
Half past three in the morning
Toss, turn, recoil; bedsit bedsheets you rewind
As his hip-hop pulsates, penetrating kitchenette walls

Half-past four…
Halting
Awkwardly
At B-Line's door
Contemplating another overcast Queens Park dawn,

If you're not careful you'll disappear through the cracks
Warns the broker of flats
Trading on inner-city housing insecurities
And trite capitalist facts
An NW10 financial crisis

Shepherding leases, deposits and contracts he fleeces
A wolf in sheep's clothing,
'Get lost!' rebuffs the tenant of 14B
'But I need my sleep.'

Burns Night

Famed tim'rous beastie
Candlelit literary lips
Utter ancient psalms
In Scotland unified
Address to the haggis
'great chieftain o' the puddin'-race'
Magical, sweet and sour, oatmeal
A Scottish dream
Burning flame

A Tale of Two Citizens

An organic café brews sophistication next to
A pawn shop flirting in desperation
A urine-soaked stairwell winds, overlooking
Victorian terraces and tree-lined decorum

From the boardroom, across from the boarded windows,
Pinstriped suits make executive decisions
Cold-shouldering hoodies *worn* with a lack of opportunities
Holding a brief case of respectability in hand

City of London crooks trade in bright futures
Whilst youngers, dealers peddle,
Grim realities on rusty BMXs

They text each other
Strictly business by Blackberry
Prescribed paths meet at the club that night
On the narcotic dusted toilet seat

With a rolled ten-pound note
They sniff hungrily at each other's coke
Kneeling, lining up for Nirvana
Swallowing bitter pills
Dancing for acceptance and release
From bad karma

The Australian Nightmare

Alas,
The Australian Dream only got as far
As the manicured lawns that dose in Caringbah
En route we raced and rioted past Cronulla's distressed
Surf and turfed out of the RSL back bar

In God's Own Shire
You hear a muffled exhaust and an immigrant's sigh
Wogboy numberplates
announce themselves in irony at the traffic lights

Yawning Sylvanian Waters
Locked up their bigoted daughters
In reali–TV
Screened privately
Moored
By a boater's sea

Saint George's River blood flows cold and indifferently
Artificially, nightclub chintzy loudspeaker houses
Blast out glam pop into the small hours

The original boatpeople
Exclude
The other boat people, as there is no room
They ashore us
An I(s)land anchored in the fears of Slyvania's soap opera
Of sons and daughters

In God's Own Country

Commuting

I. There

The moist red towel is whipped off the wintry windscreen
by the courageous, conjuring commuter
Dancing past the bull bar
Modern day matador
who anticipates today's Freeway,
He opens the car door remotely
The heavy, satisfying clunk and squash of rubber
Seals him in.

Lights click clockwise two notches forward
Mirror, signal and glance in vain
Right to a floral frosted wing mirror
He holds down the handbrake and is swiftly weighed down
Bluetooth runes switch on for connection
It is AM, 5:30am but he scans to FM news
of terrorist bombings

Switched on the Hume Highway to Redemption
Self-reinvention
He is on the commute to work

Controlled cruising past Federation houses,
Californian bungalows,
Rows of weather-boarded homes
Wood burning chimney stacks exhale
The fossil-fuelled history
He leaves Australia's First Inland City behind
Established in 1834 boasts the sign

Preserved prejudices in the aspic of absurdity
Acerbity

To the left on Sloane Street,
a ghostly Roundhouse
turns its back on a glittering history
The heater starts to thaw the faint dawning
Chorus of HGVs, beeping and reversing
Goods vans announcing deliveries

Mist in turbulence, high-beamed subservience
To swirling low-flying clouds
Shrouding the Garroorigang back road

He accelerates past the glowing M of fast food
Now parallel to the Highway
The road slips into the Hume
Cruise controls set on a tarmac jet
He flies past Kiki's at 120 km/h
Only pausing with calculated decision at Collector's cameras
to avoid number plated recognition
Slowing for bureaucratic anonymity

The darkness fades into a grey blue haze
Lake George divides the ranges
Half-way to a new identity
He sheds the skin of family responsibilities
Cocooned in suburban net-curtained certainty

Emerging a butterfly or new-aged working bee?
A hovering drone at 110 kilometres an hour
He waits for the sleepy police to follow
Twenty minutes from the Territory

On approach he weaves between rumble strips
Turning right at the concrete- under-pass
Stalled at the traffic lit gateway to Gungahlin City
Regaining speed to 80 km per hour
Galloping down the tarmac divided fields

On Horse Park Drive
Against the wave of oncoming traffic immobility
Throsby's clinically etched sterility
Carved up by throbbing bulldozers,

Pale-green grass seed, like a kale milkshake
Sprayed onto brown field's soft verges
The road yawns
Constricted roadworks opening

Into shiny Forde's façade
perfectly rendered, sharp angled geometry
Gated communities of serviced apartments
and artificial lawns

II. & Back

Home at dusk, lights on to warn wildlife
Guzzling fuel Goulburn-bound,
Cantering up Horse Park Drive
Alongside a bejewelled bead-string of headlights
Glowing like pearls in the dark night
Illuminating the pilgrim's path
The Gungahlin Tales of tailbacks

Switched off the Hume Highway to Redemption
Self-reinvention
He is on the commute back from work

The next 80 kilometres on auto-pilot,
Sealed into a podcast, hypnotised

Preserved prejudices in the aspic of absurdity
Acerbity

Established in 1834 boasts the sign

He enters Australia' First Inland City, family in mind
He decelerates past the glowing M of Highway fast food

The road slips off the Hume
Back on the Garroorigang Road

The fossil-fuelled history
Wood burning chimney stacks exhale
Rows of weather-worn homes
Californian bungalows,
Controlled cruising past Federation houses,

Mirror, signal and indication
The courageous commuter comes to a standstill
Lights click anti-clockwise two notches backward
He hauls the handbrake and is swiftly upright
Bluetooth decays
Batteries bled empty
Disconnecting all possible devices

It is PM, 5:30pm and he turns off the PM podcast
of terrorist bombings

The moist red towel placed back on the windscreen
by the gritty commuter
Dancing past the bull bar
Modern day matador,
who anticipates tomorrow's frost,
He closes the car door remotely
The heavy, satisfying clunk and squash of rubber
Seals him out

Yvette

Yvette addressed my hair busily on top
Drone hovering, humming above
Black and gold hoop earrings pendulous
She waxed lyrically, pollinated promises dripped
Nectar from the fingertips, of her tongue a pitter patter
Patois speckling the conservatory window—condensation
Warm air rising, a sing song Saturday conversation

Beeswax dextrous Queen
Worker bee waggling in dance
Hourglass figure of eight gripped
Sequined denim diamante hips
To the power of infinity ∞

Afro re-imaginings
Buzzing the cut first, shaping it up
Deftly twisting, strands golden-glossy-brown
Roots to extremities, rehydrating natty
Matted compounds, complex preparations
Beckoning dreadlocked maturations
Discussing her parlaying pardner schemes and lotteries

Fascination with her Caribbean lilt
Reminiscing, Blue Mountains misty eyes
Twinkle Ocho Rios horizon sky

Separating congas, facts from fictions, confluences of thought
Streams of consciousness
Multiple strands combined, sweeping up new undergrowth
Honeycombing hair for loose ends
With a click of her wrists, a sucking of teeth

Smiling seasoning *ital* recipes, infusing rice,
coconut milk of human kindness
Her skin a high yellow iridescence, shining hybrid example
Countenanced Chinese Jamaican undertones
Hairweave kinky, spirals DNA dizzying
Yvette, double helix of graceful influences

She waxed lyrically, whilst pollinated promises dripped
Nectar from the fingertips, of her tongue a pitter patter
Patois speckling the conservatory window—condensation
Warm air rising, a sing song Saturday conversation

HOME

(spirit / soul)

Melanin Masked White

White masked melanin
Avatars of illusion
Lightening the dark from within

Black souls constructed by white folk
Doubly conscious, born with the caul of second sight
Constricted complex-ions
Tightened tensions
Colonially manufactured neuroses

In a laboratory lined by test tubes, tied in delirium
Incoherent, de-negrification serums
Disguising appearances, de-blackening histories
Skin bleaching agents causing irritation
Ochronosis, blue-black discolouration and disease
Mercurial poisoning of pores
No pause for thought

Squeeze the pipette of pigmentocracy
With one drop of hypocrisy
Into the petri dish of dreams
Create pigments of the imagination

Commercial cosmetics of whitewashing
Noxious concoctions to conceal blemishes
Colour privileges, avatar of Western prejudice

Melanin white masked
Avatars of illusion
Darkening the light

Avatars of Darkness

In memory of Bert Williams and John Howard Griffin

Bert's avatar danced in the dark
A light skinned man daubed in war paint
Wearing a burnt cork mask
Playing the dim-witted coon
Staged his appearances for Broadway

Overwhelmed by a blackface mask
No escape from public demands
The false identity of minstrelsy

John Black Like Me
Six weeks of segregation
America in the fifties
Through southern states of degradation
Bitter skin pills to swallow

Hate stares shrivelling human souls
Branded, deprived of rights
Like livestock
Given death threats and an effigy
10th class citizenry

A Follicle Comedy

'You're hurting my hair!' repeatedly I cried
Mum brushed my afro, shaping it spherical
Topiary, producing a painful Jackson Five

Relationship with haircare temperamental
Nora Nit Nurse ruffled and picked at my 'fro
Eighties styles relaxed, realising potential

Apple gel attempts at gaining a soul glo
Soon though dried into a dandruffed breeze block
Inspired by Carl Lewis's buzz cut on podium

Without clippers, Mum's scissors failed a close crop
Thus, headlong to Cutting Corner, on a quest
for grade one back and sides below a flat top

Ephemeral, it failed the maintenance test
Soon resembling a lopsided loaf of bread
Fast forward, nineties hairstyles happened next

Scratching my head, wondering what to do instead
Baby dreads and rope twists swung into fashion
Def Row barbers mangled strands, beeswax excess

Shaved undercuts got higher, upward expansion
Resulting in the look of a pineapple
Finally, skinhead to my satisfaction

Dreadlocks nailed to wood offering three samples
Tokyo backcombed instant dreads, crochet needled
Later, I'd revert to the natural

Knitting extensions then made it grow feeble
Liberating locks undone with nappy hair
The neglect method became more feasible

Mature congos freely forming and happy
Wrapped in tams, rarely now do I have a care

Two Nanas Intertwined

Nana Ghana for the
sowing seeds, your abstract strategies in *owari*
Basket of plantain on, heading headlong to Makola Market

Nana England for your
crosswords across chasms never understood, the
cryptic clues of youth, lost, canned laughter on the box at *Alf Garnett*

Nana Ghana for the
pebble and pit of your empty stomach
Walking to the well, hell for leather soles, what a palaver

Nana England for your
cheeks cobwebbed red, tissues blue-veined tracing paper
As you watch the darts stars hit and miss their targets

Nana Ghana for the
proud Kwahu matriarch commanding compound
Looming brightly weaving *kente*, making garments

Nana England for your
bottles of bitter lemon from the larder, swigging
gin and tonic, bobby pins fixing hairnets

Nana Ghana for the
conjuring thick wooden wand, pounding up and down
Magician making fufu from plantain flour, cocoyam and cassava

Nana England for your
whisks off to whist drives in your Morris Minor
Pulling the choke stick fully so it started

Nana Ghana for the
trade in Twi, Ga, Ewe and Fante
Akan business magnate making profits

Nana England for your
stories of when you worked at William Wallace auctions
Now a pastel and watercolour retiring artist

Nana Ghana for the
fermentation of *kenkey* in a ma(i)ze of leaves, pods
of cocoa lying in sun's harvest

Nana England for your
battered board game boxes, traps for Flounders, Beetle
Drive and Happy Families for hermits

Nana Ghana for the
prayers to *Nyame* for the abundance
Of crops and cattle in your garden

Nana England for your
warm and rounded Wiltshire consonants
And vowels sounding like a mouth full of marbles

Nana Ghana for the
softly shredded airy sounds, bitonal
Akan language, nasal, tongue twisting Twi argot
Nana England for your
bone handled cutlery and polished bone china teas
Grapefruit spoon silver teardrops, without tarnish

Nana Ghana for the
chats in baby Twi with me at your side
On uneven steps of laterite, my safety harness

Nana England for your

hairspray cold to the touch in golden canisters
Shaken like maracas, spraying your beehive, nest of hornets

Nana Ghana for the
richness and resilience in your Obo home,
A Kingdom, proudly holding on to sacrifice and tribal scars

Nana England for your
cerulean piped icing on your 70th birthday
Cake of ages, snow white, candles in the darkness

Nana Ghana for the
four rooms around quadrangle courtyard
Inner sanctums filled with *Obosomfie* fetishes

Nana England for your
locks of brown hair locked in closets, silver, keys to *Narnia*
Wardrobed in aspic fifties frocks and horn-rimmed glasses

Nana Ghana for the
oily orange iridescent juice of soup
Dripping from your fingertips, stews, ground and palm nut
Nana Ghana this is for your
Plastic coated enteric orange lozenges, medicines in amber bottles
Entering, messages in bottles, sent by Nana England, for your Parkinson's
The reason in '77 we departed

Nanas this is for your stories
neon pink *Battenburg* cake slivers geometric
Fondant Fancies, Bakewell Tarts half-baked tales of natives by *Mr Kipling*, halved
Dense jungles in books, cut by Ghanaian axemanship,
staffs and crooks, pioneering and knotting borrowed by boy scouts
from Baden-Powell fighting Anglo-Ashanti Wars
Here's to peace, putting together the pieces and two nanas intertwined

Atumpan—Spiritual sounds

Akan talking drum
Accompany the dance
Open goblet forms
Drinking in the sun
Golden coastal treasure
A hit, two angular sticks
Membrane stretched
across the head
inside a metal ring
hessian string anchored
by seven conical pegs
outsides circling
One metre high on life
fifty cm diameter top
Placed, heavy on wooden
stand, at an angle, played
or fixed by two long sticks
inserted in two holes
where pegs often go,
sometimes hammered
in ground, secured by rope
made from a single piece
wood open bottomed,
narrow base mediation
in between body and mind
how you carry in parade
on head behind
a second walks behind
and plays in tune

Tuned in to each other
Low tone mother
High tone man, two
sounds sending signals
village to village
attuned Twi, Akan
large drum membrane
language, resonates low
Two sticks play
Dampening membrane
Palmed or struck
Fingertips drip with
Iridescent orange stew
Akrama master drummer
Beats Akwaaba on drums
Adorned with adinkra
ink stamped Gye Nyame,
Afenan, Adwo, Wawa aba,
Sankofa; some covered
with geometric figures,
calculated rectangles,
diamonds or painted hues
grey, blue or natural
wood, Sacred, no blood,
jawbones or skulls, made
from hard tweneboa trees,
Sacrificing eggs, Ashanti
prayers said, before felling,
telling sounds of spirits.

Web of Oddballs

Mum, dad & I
Three oddballs in a line
Brown, black and white
Bedford, Obo and Salisbury

Then came a passer-by
Spellbound by the magical sight
Strangers in Accra, abrofo in his path

Further, against the odds
Addendum to mysterious combination
An albino joined our throng
The whole world in microcosm
Adding to the drama, in paranormal panorama

The passer-by spun around
Like Anansi in retreat; giddy with disbelief
At the orb lines of life's lottery
Caught in that moment's
Web, of improbability

High Life

The planes of Hounslow roar above
the jet setting black perspiring skin
Engulfed in batakari
The hips of Highlife dancers in take off
Runaways on runways
High on life, on their own flight path
Hips and Highlife
Hips hula hooping, taxiing
Towards dancefloor trajectories
Arms calligraphic swirls of Adinkra
Envisioning symbols of Akan choreography
Shoulders swaddled in kente cloth
No re-fuelling, roiling hips don't stop
Adinkra gold chain pendants on show
Flinging skyward in song to Onyamekopon
Odo fisherman throw nets to catch their fancies
And compliments, weaving mischievously
In their kente webs, looming
Persuasive superheroes like Anansi
With the hips of tricksters conjuring,
the tricks of hipsters with rhythm
Bending down low,
Corkscrews opening sweet palm wine
In their own sweet signatures of time
Palm nut and ground nut stews in the atmosphere
Plantain caramelises the summer breeze in here
Slowly, giant snails trail in the air
Brandy roils the glass, viscous in anticipation
The brass and drums combine to tease
The diaspora into chorus
Ghanaians from Hamburg in silk shirts
and billowing MC Hammer pants join us.
Together high on life, we take off

Ventriloquist

Midwinter, sitting in a puddle of stale lager,
lips, beermat stick, stubbornly to my glass
Frozen out by my girlfriend, served my last chance
I find a bar to drown out my sorrows
Joining the mass of maudlin and morose choristers,
in the Red Lion, for benediction, unsung evensong
opposite The Delphi and Apollo

Mesmerised by sadness, I watch pensioners'
advances, in amble diagonal, from Mecca Bingo
Pilgrims, who clutch trolleys and giros
dwarfed by an Art Deco cinema, tower-ing above
Cream ceramic tiles and blue neon
glow in the dark glassy streets below

In saunters Eddie of no fixed abode
herringbone coat worn over stubbled topsoil
He stumbles but recovers, head held high,
with a pigskin rectangular briefcase tucked under his arm
This bucolic visitor to the inner city, foolhardy
gate crasher from a period drama,
set, in the Casterbridge countryside

Eddie drags the ladderback towards me, sets up camp
without invitation, he fills me in with his spiritual journeys,
on and off the beaten track, His teeth and gold chain flash
in synchrony with glitter in his eyes
Smiling, salivating he orders us a pint,
spraying me with stories of his life, regaling tales triumphant

Foam spills out from the seat cushion gash
He sits back on his threadbare throne
Eddie's eyebrows raise, triumphal archways of anticipation,
Entrances, passageways, a double invitation
to unique and compelling middle age tales:

Raised and let down on the Old Kent Road
borne to brutal paternal beatings
in the sixties, married and father at sixteen
Swallowing air and lager,
Eddie fails to quench thirst for discovery,
he continues to talk of his spirituality
I listen to him, gulp, and drink it all in

Eddie is a mendicant, seeking shelter in monasteries
a modern-day monk, He opens a flimsy plastic folder,
like a B and B foyer, stuffed with leaflets and writing
compendium of evidence answering my jury of disbelief
Fingers swooping on pages, turning
he explains his annotations are part of his book
Peregrinations soon to be published, subject to edits
subjected and freed by spiritual influences

Expounding between swills and spitting
viscous globules into his handkerchief, intermittently,
his philosophy—life's vicissitudes, vicious and kind,
out of his control, Eddie's convinced he is being helped,
taken off one path onto another,
He twists his half full empty glass,
his current good fortune, a result of divine interventions

Back to his childhood, he had visions of his grandfather at 11
Told by his father he was a dunce, cornered
Eddie confesses he learned to read and write latterly,
righted in his late forties

Suddenly with a grin as broad as his brogue,
he opens up his Pandora's box
sliding the latches, pressing the golden buttons,
remote and controlled slow motion stagecraft
Eddie rests his pint glass, choreographed for his audience,
part of a script often performed
He throws his voice around the room
Laughter from his belly, volcano erupting *venter*,
roaring *gastro* lava, stomach echoes
above and beyond the pub jukebox

Appearing out of theatrical curtain
From the crushed velveteen burgundy,
like a rabbit from a magician's hat,
out comes his party trick:

A ventriloquist's dummy!
Funnily, sitting it familiarly on his lap
I sit dumbfounded, dummy struck
Picked up somewhere on his turnpike travels
Eddie had kept it as a sign of good luck

So, I sit entranced, two dummies with Eddie, caught in the eddy
Spider webbed stale froth beading beer glasses
Listening to his ebb and flow, *loquacious*, palavers
Lubricated and lightened by lager, it is my round
The public house puppeteer brings tears to my eyes,
tugging heartstrings with the tension of his stories
Again, Eddie talks of karma,
He elucidates, gains all given back in some way,
we are all primed for something else

Hypnotised by prophet Pythia in a Kilburn pub
Priest worshipping at the Red Lion temple,
across the road from the Apollo, visitation by
the Delphic Oracle in battered brogues

his herringbone sleeve, decorated leather patch elbow
wipes froth, off his face and chin,

Perhaps God was speaking through Him
Inner city, midwinter, ventriloquist

Kilburn High Road Stroll

A late afternoon stroll on the Kilburn High Road
In tune with cosmopolitan calypso
Patois on the pavements
Domino slapping statements
How I long to come back home

Pawnbrokers and Poundland
In this lost and nearly new-found land
Boots, Primark and Ladbrokes
Turf accountant chair rows
Lined up in a convoy of hope
Betting slips left, screwed up in distress

A late afternoon stroll on the Kilburn High Road
In tune with cosmopolitan calypso
Patois on the pavements
Domino slapping statements
How I long to come back home

I make hasty chase for the 96 bus
Past Somali telecommunications in a rush
that offer money transfer,
take me back
to my inner-city crush

A late afternoon stroll on the Kilburn High Road
In tune with cosmopolitan calypso
Patois on the pavements
Domino slapping statements
How I long to come back home

Halal butchers face Mecca
Opposite the street beggars
In a heartbeat I'll feast
At Chicken Cottage with chips
Savouring those days, I lick my lips

A late afternoon stroll on the Kilburn High Road
In tune with cosmopolitan calypso
Patois on the pavements
Domino slapping statements
How I long to come back home

Winding down at Willesden Lane
In the tropical heat of Vijays
Marinating on curried meat and dosai
Smelling the spice of life
of days gone by

A late afternoon stroll on the Kilburn High Road
In tune with cosmopolitan calypso
Patois on the pavements
Domino slapping statements
How I long to come back home

I'll wash it all down, with a few pints of stout
Calling last orders, The Kilburn Tavern
slurs and spills out
Fag-ends aglow with the glitter of Black Gold
Time to go with the flow

A late afternoon stroll on the Kilburn High Road
In tune with cosmopolitan calypso
Patois on the pavements
Domino slapping statements
How I long to come back home

The thirsty are quenched
Their ashtrays unearthed
Abandoned tables are upturned
Joining the dinner and dance drumbeat
Dancers off their faces and feet.

A late afternoon stroll on the Kilburn High Road
In tune with cosmopolitan calypso
Patois on the pavements
Domino slapping statements
How I long to come back home

Time to leave the scene
Under the bridge at Brondesbury
Ticket scalpers recycle Oyster cards
They reel in at the Jubilee Line
Forcing open tightly clenched palms
Of their gold, silver and brass

A late afternoon stroll on the Kilburn High Road
In tune with cosmopolitan calypso
Patois on the pavements
Domino slapping statements
How I long to come back home

Haibun8

Haibun-One

Goulburn, Southern Tablelands, New South Wales, Australia. Land of extremes. Cycle of hibernation. Sheltering from the heat and swelter of stinking hot forty-degree days, mosquitoes, spiders and snakes in Summer. In Winter there is hibernation from the bitter frosts and icy winds from southern tableland tops and alpine mountains in the south.

Haibun-Two

Smoke envelopes bush
Embers threatening to raze
Precarious plans

Haibun-Three

The catastrophic 2020 bushfires came close to home. A neighbour explained that they had a water pump and hose in readiness to defend their property. The summer was spent trying to hibernate from the smoke haze which entered our living rooms, literally. Wind blew the smoke in from nearby bushfires. It lasted for months. We couldn't see the sun. It reminded us how near the danger was.

Haibun-Four

Father and son cutting then stacking wood in their shed as a yearly ritual, part of the rhythm of life, strange and mysterious to an outsider, a recent blow-in from the UK. When I first arrived in Goulburn in July, at the tail-end of the winter of 2010, I remember the acrid air. I had not expected wood fires to burn so fiercely. I was used to the preponderance of central heating in London. Here 'in the sticks' of a country town, wood was burnt for warmth, hibernation. Burnt fog. Tarnished air.

Haibun-Five

Wood-stack balancing
Ready for hibernation
Father-son prepare

Haibun-Six

Slip, slap, slop non-stop
Melanoma prevention
Shady existence

Haibun-Seven

I spent most of the time chasing the sun when I was in the UK. As a child I remember trying to warm myself up in my parent's conservatory in summer, like a human solar panel. Now I escape the sun as much as possible. Hibernating in the chill of air-conditioned malls in the summertime, transported there by air-conditioned car. The skin cancer preventing mantra of 'slip slap slop'. The donning of broad brimmed hats and sunglasses.

Haibun-Eight

Barbecues inside!
Creepy crawlies advance
Australian 'Dream'

Culture shock: the first and subsequent barbecues I attended in Australia involved the cooking of the food outside but the eating of it *inside*. My myth of enjoying the great outdoors was compromised by the myriad of wildlife who wanted to share the meal with me, and of course there was the sun... (Winter and summer. Land of extremes. Hibernation habits, impossible to break.)

Nyankopoxyican Breath of Fresh Air

'We can't breathe!'
cried the diasporic seeds on barren soils
Signals sent by those tethered
to Africa, Europe and the Americas
Inhospitable stormy weather
Picked up on marine radar radio
by Deep Sea Drexciyan Dwellers
Riding high under waves of isolation
In a Bubbled Metropolis
Travelling on Aquabahn in Cruiser Control

'We can't breathe!'
Weak breath signals picked up
In Africa, Europe and the Americas
Inhospitable stormy weather

Progeny of those labelled sick and disruptive
Thrown off foul scented slave ships
on their Middle Passages
They swam from their mothers' wombs, learning to breathe
to found subaqueous empires and freshwater trajectories
Formed deep seated civilisations beneath
a vast dark abyss
created by transatlantic slavery
Brave, alternative histories

'We can't breathe!'
Weak breath signals picked up
In Africa, Europe and the Americas
Inhospitable stormy weather

Valiantly escaping through aqua worm holes
Enslaved removals evolved into wave-jumpers,
stingray and barracuda battalions
to Positron Island, Bubble Metropolis, Danger Bay
Reaching Drexciya in stages
Evolutionary deep Black Atlantic Ocean navigation
An aquazone surrounding isolated archipelago

'We can't breathe!'
Weak breath signals picked up
In Africa, Europe and the Americas
Inhospitable stormy weather

The next Drexciyan Quest:
Communicate to save land lumbered souls
from the prison industrial complex, colonisation,
decolonisation, institutional racism, post industrialisation,
macro and micro-aggressions,
global warming oppression

'We can't breathe!'
Weak breath signals picked up
In Africa, Europe and the Americas
Inhospitable stormy weather

They sent sonic invasions
From their underwater techno-pirate-stations
Helping those struggling to survive
Adverse, intense climatic changes
Attacking the mainstream of airwaves
Allowing oppressed souls to breathe

A rescue mission dreamt up by Drexciyan R.E.S.T
Research, Experimentation, Science and Technology
New systems to allow breathing were developed
In the tropos-, stratos-, mesos-, thermos-

and eventually exospheres
Finally, flying, releasing estranged cousins,
from the effects of transatlantic slavery
Breathing

'We can breathe!'
In deep sea and space

Terrestrial, seabed to exospheric adaptation
Travelling dimensional portals,
jumping-holes at liminal crossroads
Neo-evolution from Drexciyan to Nyankopoxican
Extra-terrestrial storm weathering then harnessing

Formation of a single, continuous superfield
Hybrid reality, mediating all mass, space, time and energy
Innovative Molecular Enhancement Technologies
The stolen plotting liberation after surviving
abject global conditioning
Deep in the ocean, on land and air

Soul survivors, regrouping,
readying for the Journey Home (Future)
Wherever we choose to go

A Bass Drum Talks of its Ancestors

A burst of sudden tempo evokes tremors
Traumatic memories, painful and celebratory,
Repercussions
Slow down,
as the trad theorists say: *lento, largo*
Step on it *andante,*
or else you'll break my skin
putting your metal foot pedal heavily, my covering is thin
I come from a fine blue veined line of royal genealogy, protecting royalty
Housed in sacred dwellings, in palaces, ceremoniously announcing rituals
Births, deaths and marriages, my Akan ancestors talked languages from within
A historic smartphone communicating
Beat viciously, stirring excitement and passion, prelude to warrior battle
Sounding ancient notifications, alertness, entertainment
Mimicking, imitating rhythms and intonations
Syllabic tones reinvented on drummed skin
Inflected messages on a tri-tonic scale with pitch regulation
You see, I'm still a talking drum of sorts, have some respect
My forebears had an hour-glass figure, two heads connected,
made tense by cords of leather,
Squeezed by griots between arm and body
To create human speech prosody
Tempo rubato, you see, time has been robbed from me
If only you and the audience make the right choice: listen to hear
rubato rhythms, inclined ears exalt.

Acknowledgements

Grateful acknowledgment is made to the editors and staff of the following magazines and websites, in which versions of these poems originally appeared:

'Dandelion Diaspora' appeared in *Alien, Winter Edition, Issue 8* (Fly on the Wall Press, 2021)

'Melanin Masked White' appeared in Poor Yorick Literary Journal, Special Issue: Masks, (April 2021)

'My Golden Coast' appeared in *The Best New British and Irish Poets Anthology 2019-2021*, The Black Spring Press Group

'The Writing on the Wall' was featured as The Sunday Poem and was published on the *Afropean* website (2020)

'Rich Genetic Commonwealth' was broadcast by *Golden Walkman Magazine* (Literary Magazine/ podcast), 'Survivor' Themed Issue, (January 2021)

'Blossom' appeared in *the flower shop on the corner* Anthology, Red Penguin Books (March 2021)

'Wake Up Call' appeared in *dyst Literary Journal*, Issue 5, 31 March 2021, RoseyRavelston Bookshop & Publishing Services (March 2021)

'Nyankopoxyican Breath of Fresh Air' first appeared in *Nombono Anthology– Speculative Poetry by BIPOC Poets,* Sundress Publications, ed Akua Lezli Hope, October 2021.

About the Author

Andrew Geoffrey Kwabena Moss is a writer and teacher who has lived in the UK, Japan and currently Australia. Of Anglo-Ghanaian heritage, his work seeks to explore and challenge liminal landscapes, complex identities and the social constructs of race. He has been published in numerous international journals, and has received several awards, including two Best of Net Awards, a Pushcart Prize, and a Rhysling Award nomination.

Most recently, his work has featured in several anthologies, including *The Best New British and Irish Poets Anthology 2019-2021*, *Poetry for the Planet* and *Nombono: An Anthology of Speculative Poetry by BIPOC Poets*.

Andrew's debut novella *Nicked Names* was published by RoseyRavelston Books in July 2022. He released three full length poetry books *Japanabandon*, *Manifest.oh!* and *Diaspora³* through RoseyRavelston Books in February 2023.

In 2023, he was commissioned as a Red Room Poetry 30in30 artist in association with the National Gallery of Australia, writing an ekphrastic poem 'HHH/KKK' in response to Fiona Foley's photograph 'HHH'.

Andrew's fourth poetry collection *Objections, Scars & Artefacts* was published by RoseyRavelston Books in October 2023.

www.ingramcontent.com/pod-product-compliance
Ingram Content Group Australia Pty Ltd
76 Discovery Rd, Dandenong South VIC 3175, AU
AUHW020639050325
407891AU00002B/17